I0494671

A small book by Julie Osaretin Osayanoe .

A husband is certainly not the father of a child, or the man a woman is accidentally standing with, and just because of shame , during introductions to some old classmates or some other persons not known good enough fits in as being called a husband. According to the dictionary, a husband is a married man considered in relation to his spouse.

My name is Goldie and I am a successful woman. For me, success means more than having a carrier and being rich. Success means being married. After so much youthful exuberances and so many vices, I am forced to make a choice between a number of men I have in the past, in one way or the other, introduced as my husband. Dear readers please advise me on whom to choose as a husband now that I am about to make it official otherwise I 'll remain a married woman on the lips only, without marriage certificate. Please read my story....

We were a group of four friends. Every day after school, we'd play some game called "Would you take my gold or silver" and so it goes

"Would you take my gold or silver,

Gold or silver (twice)

Would you take my gold or silver, my dear lady"?

Eliza and I will normally will sing while clapping our hands and Ebitemi and Kiki simultaneously dances round us in a circle. Whoever is being caught up in our midst is asked to choose between gold or silver...

 Ebitemi always chose gold and she always ended up on my side. Eliza on the other hand was called "Silver" and Kiki always ended up behind her. On this day, I had just finished playing with Eliza,

Ebitemi and Kiki when I suddenly decided to go home. On getting home, I heard some music on the radio in pidgin English

"If I finish my school cert. (short for school certificate),

I will marry Johnny,

oh Johnny take me home,

to be your lovely wife, blab blaaa."

Although still young, this music was one of my favourite songs on radio. It made me to take a brighter look at the future ahead as regards getting married to a man, and not just to any man, to the one man I would love.

While at the primary school, I had a crush on Kessington. Kessington was a very tall young boy who registered late at the Baptist primary School where I attended. I really didn't know what was special about him, maybe because his uniforms were new, or maybe because he was tall. He was the tallest amongst the boys though. His parents had just recently moved in from another town.

I couldn't take my eyes off him. I thought about him during school hours. At home, when the music played on the radio, I would change Johnny to Kess and sing loudly. On a particular day, unknown to me, my mum was watching me. She watched me carefully dance and sing my heart out and then eventually switched off the radio.

"Too soon my dear!" she said in amazement.

"Oh no mama, I want to have this idea now in my head otherwise I may forget quickly" I replied sheepishly.

I was preparing to get baptized because I wasn't baptized as an infant so I usually attended the catechism classes every Saturday evening and It was worse off at the catechism classes with the presence of Johnny. Kess lived far away, I never saw him in church, rather another young boy called Johnny. I didn't really like Johnny because he used to wear glasses. The glasses made him look years older. He liked me and always wanted to take his seat next to mine, I was his girl crush.

Before the catechism classes started, we usually sang the song

"Jesus loves the little children

All the children of the world

They are yellow, black and white,

They are precious in His sight

Jesus loves the little children of the world"

My own version of this song was different. I'd changed the song to

"Jesus loves the little children

All the children of the world

They have bad eyes and good eyes,

They are precious in His sight

Jesus loves the little children of the world"

Bad eyes….referring to Johnny…I wasn't happy with his taking his seat close to mine. Eventually he stopped. So he isn't mentioned in my love world. In my love world, each man (my lovers) involved will be receiving a nickname and these nicknames will depend on what these lovers of mine knows best.

Kiki was our next door neighbour. She was also my classmate and her elder brother was already in the secondary school while we were still at the primary school. His name was Kenneth, (the K Family). He liked me a lot, he used Kiki's friendship with me as an avenue to get closer to me;

In fact the very first love letter I received came from Ken (Mr. Romantic).

These were the words

Dear Goldie

Words cannot express what I feel each time I see you. Have you ever asked yourself why I came regularly to fetch water at your house even though the chores of fetching water was meant for Kiki? It was just to see your beautiful face. You are the sugar in my tea, and the only roach in my cupboard (she laughs haahaahaa) and the every breath I take! And at the end he draws a flower, a hibiscus flower like this one below

The flower was white in colour without its stem.
Finally he writes at the end "when we finally make

love, we shall both colour this flower red, which would be a symbol of our love for each other and the green stem, our kids would draw and colour that, to show a sign of our productivity".

He wrote this then and many more letters which he usually posted to me through his sister Kiki. What romantic! .Ken was so romantic, at his age, he knew a lot already about romance and sexual relationships. This is by the way.

Then comes the Pharmacy where my mum buys medications whenever any of my siblings took ill. The sales boy at the Pharmacy also had his eyes on me; Each time I went to get some paracetamol or some other medications that were not so expensive, he would gladly ask me to take it for free. What benevolence from Iyke (Mr. Benevolence).

And finally the son (Bright) of a Supermarket owner where we bought beverages every morning whenever we ran out of some at home. On a particular day, Bright offered me a lot of chocolates and biscuits. I refused this offer and many more without actually knowing why. Although he was generous (Mr. Generous), but something kept holding me back. With the sales boy at the pharmacy, it was a different ball game altogether.

20years on, after these youthful exuberances, I am still not married. Even though at this stage of my life, I am a very successful woman. How is success defined anyway without marriage? According to my opinion and my experiences, a successful woman might have everything to include money, carrier, kids and without being married is not respected except maybe she is a nun.

All through the years of my life, I have been involved with several men and it was convenient to introduce them as my husbands.

Going down memory lane.

On my 18th birthday, I was with Mr. Romantic Ken. He would always write his love letters, "several copies of which I kept". He was my kind of man, sometimes I ask myself why? I love romance. I love men who adore women with all the beautiful words in the world even when they didn't have money to buy gift or flowers, they just show love.

Kiki had free entrance into my home, so it made it easier for us to communicate and on my birthday, his card and love letter number 156 was the very first thing I received. In it he already painted our love world and invited me for a romantic lunch at his house. Although, I was forewarned by the red coloured hibiscus flower which we were both supposed to colour together, I still did fall for this trap. I was carried away by the flower painting . It was there I lost my innocence. Unforgettable. He was my first love amongst the other men I mentioned earlier.

I gained admission into the university and it was there I met a Ghanaian who had a vintage shop by the university gate. At the shop, he sold high quality ladies wears and some second hand clothes commonly called *"okrika"* then (*Nigerian slang*: meaning second hand clothes). His name was Benjamin Martin (Mr. Helper). He was the one who was meant to complete my story or perhaps maybe not, who knows.

This verse of the bible (Psalm 87 verse 5)

"But of Zion it shall be said, "This one and that one were born in her"; And the Most High Himself will establish her" pricks my heart.

Till today, I regard this verse of the bible as speaking to me , because I always prayed that God would send me a man who is just like me, someone who was born in me, I prayed that God Himself establishes me especially concerning marriage. For me, this verse meant that each of these men were born in me" and at a particular time in my life, they played the role of my husband.

I would regularly visit Ben's shop, even though I had nothing to buy. He was handsome and he had this gentle and sweet calming voice. His voice was actually one of the source of attraction then. A lot of girls trooped in regularly into his shop, but whenever I arrived, he stands to attend to my needs. Often times, he never had what I needed in his shop.

After my graduation from the university, I travelled to the state where I was posted for my

N.Y.S.C. In Nigeria, N.Y.S.C stands the National Youth Service Corps and during the service year (which is usually a period of one year), Corpers are meant to serve the Nigerian nation in their various disciplines.

I was sent to serve at the hospital. Unbeknown to me, Ken also worked there. Although he was my first love, we lost contact because his family moved to another state.

His father was an army officer, so he and his family relocated to Benue state where I was also posted for my youth service. All through the years, I had forgotten about Ken, but this day, those sweet memories came back. We met at the hospital entrance where we both worked. He worked there as an optometrist. I was assigned to work in the laboratory. He never took me to his house one day. The hospital had a lodge, so had the NYSC. We continued our romance there at the hospital or the Corper's lodge . I introduced him to my fellow Corp members' friends as my husband. No one at the hospital told me anything about him until I told them I was pregnant. Ken was married and his wife (a medical doctor) had travelled overseas on a course so it was convenient for him to have me.

He always shoved me off each time I would pose the question about his marital status. He did it because he wasn't sure his wife would come back and he was still madly in love with me.

I couldn't have an abortion, I just had to keep this child. I was ashamed to travel back home after the service year. Instead of travelling back to my state after completing the service year, I travelled with my Corper girlfriend to her home town, a village in south-eastern Nigeria. It was there I met the pharmacy sales boy Iyke again.

It was just a coincidence. The vehicle we took made a stop by a pharmacy because the driver had diarrhoea. As the call pulled over, I used the opportunity to stretch myself by accompanying the driver to the pharmacy. I also needed some medications too.

Iyke had grown into a very handsome man. It was during our conversation together that I learnt he had gone back to school to study Pharmacy. He was later to become the father of my second child and my second husband.

He was so excited to see me that he told the driver of the car to proceed without me. He took my bags into his pharmacy shop. After the close of the day, he took me to his house. It was there Iyke introduced me to his family as his wife. Excitement made him forget about the issue on ground.

His family has been pressuring him to marry Onyin, a native girl that they kept for him all the while he was away to study abroad. It was this same family of his that helped me through the birth of my first child and because of that I promised I would give him a child of his own; in thanksgiving for what he did for me.

Even though we were not yet married and there were no papers to show as an act of marriage, we lived as a couple.

The only barrier was language, (Nigeria has more than 500 spoken languages and the Igbo language is one of them). His family would always insult me in their language and they never really liked me because according to them, I was not from their tribe and it would be unfair that their very rich and educated brother would take all his wealth back to my state after marriage.

In fact his family poisoned his heart against mine and they made him see reasons why he shouldn't settle down with me.

As usual, on one of the beautiful mornings, we greeted each other.

"Good morning beauty", he said kissing me on the cheek.

"Good morning handsome, where are you off to this early? And why are you dressed traditionally?" I asked.

"Oh, my dear, I am off to the family meeting, it is very important." He replied, never saying what it was all going to be about.

"Ok, dear, see you later," I concluded.

It was at the family meeting they told him that I was a stranger, and that if he is forbidden to marry an Osu (*Osu* are a group of people deemed property of the gods, and relationships with these sets of people were forbidden, even till this day), why won't they forbid him to marrying me?

My question then was, is this not one Nigeria? Little did I know that sooner or later I would be travelling to another part of the world where discrimination was at the highest (as experienced by Kessington) .

It took long before he came back from the family meeting. After the meeting, he'd first visited his friend and trustee Mr. Ogbonna to seek his advice.

Mr. Ogbonna was present at the naming ceremony of my son. He was closer to Iyke than the other family members were, so his word and advice would be trusted in this relationship of ours. Obviously they had a very long discussion before he suddenly made up his mind about me. And whatever discussion they had, blew his mind.

"Welcome back my husband," I greeted, while serving his favourite meal of *fufu* and *ofe-owerri* soup.

In fact, I had made this soup specially to introduce my newly conceived child and announce my pregnancy to him.

Initially greeting or welcoming him like that made him happy because it gave him an idea that he belonged to me and we belonged to each other. "Sense of belonging to each other" made the difference for him.

Even though he didn't pay my bride price yet, to him I was his wife. But after this family meeting, his mood changed. He didn't only ignore me, he threw my food away in the bin.

"What's going on?" I questioned.

"Are you questioning me in my own house?" He replied.

"How do you think I will take care of your bastard child?" He continued.

"Bastard child?" I replied.

"Why are you acting so strange, my love? Was it not the same you who told me about the 'Oyinbo (*Nigerian slang*: meaning white, foreign) mentality'?" I continued in a very calmed manner and tone.

"Why are you addressing me as if you are an illiterate Goldie" ?

The first time he ever mentioned my name. Then I had to buckle up, because things didn't seem nice anymore. His utterances to me made it clear that it was over.

So all these while, his family members were pretending to have liked and welcomed me. At the family meeting they told him I had to go in search of the man who made me pregnant. They failed to see the true love which existed between us.

Oh, my world is crumbled, I wept bitterly. What do I do now? I sweated profusely. My body shook suddenly. It was when I told him I was pregnant for my second child he replied me that Onyin was also pregnant. I wept and cried my eyes out.

Who is Onyin, if I may ask?

Onyin is the girl I introduced as my cousin, my uncle's daughter, he replied..

"Heeee, I screamed, so you igbos (Iyke was an Igbo man, from the eastern part of Nigeria) have not changed (although not all are like that).

First you introduce a man or woman as your brother or sister and there after these persons become your sex partners.

Oh, ok; I have heard you , my father actually warned me about this igbo culture, I didn't listen, now it was time to go back home," I replied in annoyance.

"I can't be maltreated anymore," I continued, while packing up my belongings from the house we once both shared.

I left Iyke with a 3-month old pregnancy and my 1year old son.

Before I left, I thanked him for all the wonderful time we shared and also for the kindness he showed me and my son. He offered to take us in his car and drop us off at the village car park so we could travel back home. I refused.

I carried only a few of our stuff on my head and held my son in my hand. We walked a few distance and then another family member of Iyke's stopped and offered us a lift.

I accepted this time because the load on my head was very heavy and it seemed as if it was going to rain.

All through the journey I kept mum.

Mr. Chike had continually asked about my destination, I ignored him. He was coming from the family meeting too and he'd pretended as if he didn't know what was going on.

On getting to the car park, I thanked him and we left his sight.

It was on my journey back to my state, I met another unfamiliar face who called out to me at the car park.

Even though he didn't remember my name, he remembered me as Ken's wife.

"Ken's wife, how are you? Madam, hello, hello," he repeated while running towards my direction.

He shouted repeatedly.

I didn't answer at first because of the so much pain and bitter mood I was in. I didn't know whom he was calling at , talk less of being someone's wife.

The unfamiliar face was Fidelis.

Fidelis came closer and tapped me.

"Hello," he said.

"Don't you remember me? Are you not Ken's wife?"

He went on.....

"We were fellow Corpers in Benue state. You introduced some man to us then as your husband. Actually that was the first time I met with you at the camp; How are you guys and where are you heading?"

Oh, I remember now, "Hello", I returned,

"We are travelling back to my state," I answered.

Coincidentally he was also travelling to my state because his brother was a parish priest in one of the catholic churches in my state.

It was after he finished saying that and my hearing about catholic church that I burst into tears. I remembered church again, I had totally forgotten about church after all these years.

I narrated my story to him and further explained how I have not been home since after our youth service in Benue state and how I had two kids (one in the womb) with two different men who were never really married to me.

"Boooooooooh," I cried tears and wept bitterly that I attracted attention.

People around started looking at us. It was then he walked with me to another quite corner at the car park so we could have a chat.

"So you didn't marry Ken? How come you introduced him to us as your husband then?"

Anyway, problems aside, he told me softly it was ok and he thought it wise that I didn't travel home to my family because of the shame and disrespect it will bring.

He advised me on attending a crusade being organized by the church and while there he would ask his brother priest to assist in accommodating me. I needed counselling, my heart was boiling.

I hesitated at first but later agreed to his proposal.

We travelled together and on reaching the parish, his brother Christopher turned out to be one of the seminarians then at my former parish when I was very young.

The then brother Christopher visited our youth meetings regularly. I was the treasurer of the Catholic Youth Organization in my parish. Even though at that moment in my life, I have lost integrity and pride, I couldn't ever lose the idea of being a catholic, never.

At a first glance, it seemed as if I was dreaming. Fr. Christopher was celebrating the holy mass when we arrived. We waited outside for the mass to finish before seeing him. I knelt down outside the church building while the mass was being celebrated. I felt so unworthy to take a seat in the church.

I knelt down with my eyes closed and my head bowed to the ground, not noticing when Fr. Christopher walked to me and lifted me up from the ground. My total face was soaked in tears. I wanted the grounds to open so I entered inside.

Several years earlier I had told him about the opportunities of applying for a scholarship to study abroad. Then, we (brother Christopher and some other youths) would go on the internet and apply for available online scholarships. We often received scholarships forms from schools in Australia, (Newcastle upon Tyne), I will never forget those days.

The then seminarian always assisted in sending these filled in applications by post and we usually received replies that we have been granted admissions. The only obstacle then was that we weren't granted scholarships but we were always asked to pay so much as thousands of Australian dollars to be able to study abroad.

For me it was very impossible because of my poor background, although I was named *Gold* by my parents, my name couldn't pay for my education.

I went through school in a very tough way.

Back to the now, Fr. Christopher, the parish priest of the church we visited.

He hugged me and greeted me so warmly, his brother was amazed.

"So you guys know each other, what a small world!" he concluded.

"Please could you leave us alone, I have some confessions to make." I told Fidelis while leading my son towards him.

"Okay, let me take your son so I get him something to drink." Fidelis offered.

"How did you meet my brother Fidelis? Is he the father of your child?" Fr. Christopher asked...

"Oh no Fr.," I replied.

"We were fellow corpers in Benue state, sorry I am the one making the introductions.

I met him on my way home and he told me about the crusade that is being organized here tonight. I came for help."

I started crying again, "Booooooooooooooh".

"Stop crying sister, you are in the house of God the Provider and Helper.

I am all ears," he concluded.

I then narrated the story of my life to him, including how I have introduced two men as my husbands and one of them is known to his brother Fidelis.

"What a pity, what do you want us to do now?"

"Us?" I replied...

"No.....please," I continued. "It is me, I have put myself in this mess, I only need God's help and direction now, if not too late."

"Oh no sister, it is never late with God. God has plans for each of us, it is only left for us to know what these plans are.

You came at the right time and to the right place. My only fear is how we would start to narrate this painful story of yours to your parents knowing fully well that they are devout Catholics.

Anyway, I have a family committee here in this parish. I will ask the Chairpersons to accompany me to visit your family so that we do not cause drama at your place.

Meanwhile, let's get you and your son Ngozi something to eat." Iyke had named my son Ngozi. I wanted to change his name but Fr. Christopher persuaded me not to.

"There is always a reason we are in different places at different times of our lives," Fr. Christopher pointed out.

"Come to think of it, what if Iyke didn't send you packing? You won't meet me today and I want to say that the most important reason we are meeting now is about a scholarship program in Switzerland."

He went on….

 "A foreign priest came here to serve mass some years ago, then I was the assistant parish priest. He got so interested in the youth activities and he promised that when he got

back to his country, he would ask the university over there to send scholarships to study abroad to some well deserving youths in the parish. Each year we receive scholarship

forms for undergraduate studies. Unfortunately of rather fortunately this year, they had only scholarship programs for master's studies.

At the moment in the parish, there are no university graduates that is why I invited Fidelis here to ask if he was interested in studying for his master's degree abroad.

Knowing how deeply you were involved in parish youth activities back then in Warri, what more can I say that you are a very eligible candidate for this scholarship program also."

"Congratulations my dear"....Fr Christopher said in smile.

"Cheer up sister"....he went on.

"Thank you" ...I replied.

We had to send our academic transcripts to the university to enable them in Switzerland know if we were qualified to begin a master's program. Fidelis and I filled in the forms

and we got admitted.

It was testimony and thanks giving time for me at the church.

"Praise the Lord!"

The congregation replied "Amen". Unfortunately it was lent, no Alleluia's at the Lenten period, it would have been so ideal for me to sing Alleluia to my God, the GREATEST MASTERPLANNER!

This is the name I call him today for planning my life, I told the congregation listening to me attentively.

It was my thanks giving mass and I told the people present at the mass that It was proper for every Christian to give thanks to God especially for blessings received because in thanking God, we show our appreciation by telling Him how grateful we are and we make rooms open for more blessings.

I was giving a testimony in honour of what God did for me. Even though I couldn't tell the congregation every detail of my story, I just wanted to appreciate and show how grateful I was for giving my Life to God.

"Each one of us should give God a name in our lives. Today I call God the *GREATEST MASTERPLANNER*. There are wedding planners, party events planners but God can never be compared to any of these.

"Which name would you call God in your life? Have you ever received a miracle?"

" God is waiting for you to call Him your own thought-out name,

 my dear brothers and sisters in Christ" I concluded.

I got admitted into a university in Switzerland and the parish priest asked in the parish for donations for me to enable me study abroad.

Even though it was a scholarship, we needed to have some pocket money with us. A well-meaning and well- to- do parishioner offered to pay all the remaining expenses including visa and ticket fees besides the tuition which was free for us. We were really grateful.

I rushed back to my family in tears with my two kids, (one on my hand and the other in my womb) from separate fathers and asked my mother especially to forgive me. The priest and the family committee chairpersons travelled home with me to help me reconcile with my family.

It wasn't easy at first but the only good news is that I wasn't going to be around as a single mother so our neighbours do not ask questions about my marital status. I was travelling abroad away from the shame and disrespect. Having kids without getting married is shameful in our own part of the world.

My mom took care of Ngozi while I travelled to Switzerland with my unborn child.

The plane tickets we bought were a little bit expensive, I didn't mind. Fidelis insisted we paid for cheaper tickets so we travelled through another country into Switzerland. I objected because I was pregnant.

Even though the prices of the tickets we purchased were rather on the high side, we paid to have comfort throughout our journey.

 It was at the Airport's baggage claim area that I met Kessington. He was in Switzerland from Nigeria on a different flight.

According to him, he was abroad all these years after we left secondary school. He had grown into a very tall gentleman and while we left secondary school , he got into a team of basketball players, he got lucky and travelled abroad. First to the US and then back to Switzerland. He met his wife Ana, a white woman while playing basketball in the US. She was a student (on exchange program) at the college where Kessington played.

Even though I was 7 months gone in my pregnancy, he could still recognize me because of my face. According to him, there was none other like my face, it was beautiful.

My thoughts immediately drifted away. I started reminiscing on my beauty. I cannot take credits for my beauty but I am really beautiful, even though I didn't have to make up artificially, my face was naturally made up.

I stood regularly in front of the mirror often times to ask why such a beautiful woman like me would still be unmarried at this time of my life after two imaginary husbands.

"Anyway, good to see you," he exclaimed. My thoughts came back. I quickly wiped up my face gently to make sure I wasn't dreaming.

"Y'all look good?" He continued in an American accent.

"I just flew in from Nigeria on Lufthansa Air, how come I didn't see y'all on the flight?" He questioned.

It was at that moment Fidelis came telling me our travelling bags were on another platform different from where I stood and coincidentally met Kess,

"Is that your husband?" Kess asked.

"No," I replied……

I told him no but I have a lot of stories to tell.

"I am here to study and you? What is your situation now?"

"Oh, I am happily married, although it has not be quite peaceful due to the high levels of racisms here." He answered.

"I have two kids, I just visited home recently to ask my father to name my first son."

"Hmm," I sighed.

"What is all the sighing about? You are heavy and you are not happy?

Do you know how long it took my wife to get pregnant?"

'Not that Kess, there is more to life than you think"... I replied.

"But please we would be needing your assistance here, first to get to our student hostel and then to learn the life style here"... I continued.

Meanwhile, Ana and their two kids were already waiting to pick him up. Ana's family wasn't there because they weren't very fond of Kess because of his being black. Though Ana's family objected to their getting married, Ana's persistence made the wedding take place. And because of this, Kess vowed that Ana would be his first wife forever.

Kess introduced Ana to me and told us to wait at one of the restaurants at the airport while he drove his wife and kids back home.

He came back later to the airport to pick us to the university. Kess is from my tribe.

We excused ourselves from Fidelis so we could speak in our own mother tongue on the way to the university.

I explained to him all that has transpired ...... and how bitter I was till God helped me now to come abroad and study.

"*Shuooo*,(an Urhobo tribe slang showing how surprised someone is) You mean all these things happened to you?" He replied.

It was during our conversation that he told me he knew about my girl crush on him. He went further to say that he found the little notes I used to write about being in love with him while we were at school.

It was sad that he couldn't reciprocate my love back then. He had also pictured himself as my husband and regularly fantasized about being that even though we didn't have time to be in a relationship.

"I hope you don't mind now if I introduce you as my husband here in this community?" I chipped in quickly in our language.

It was then we both laughed and he replied "Not at all".

We arrived at the University and we met some other black students like us who travelled from other cities in Nigeria to study too.

We introduced ourselves and again, I quickly introduced Kess as my husband. I didn't want people (especially among the black Nigerian students gossips that may arise sooner or later) asking questions.

Fidelis was a little bit amazed and perplexed. I warned him to keep this secret between us.

"Why are you doing this?" Fidelis asked.

"I do not know, my brother, I don't know, and especially now I don't even know why I had ran into Kess in the first place," I answered.

"You remember we were supposed to get a different flight ticket because of being cheap?

If not that I insisted we travelled with the more expensive one, we wouldn't run into Kess.

Maybe it is for this reason." I concluded.

To the Switzerland black student community in the campus was Kess my husband.

He visited me regularly and made sure I registered for the right insurance facilities to include my unborn child. He was well informed about the laws in Switzerland.

I delivered my child after two months of arrival and I was giving some months off from the study program to enable to take care of my new born Elina.

Kess visited regularly although it pained him that my daughter couldn't bear his last name so that inquisitive people do not ask further questions.

According to him, it would be a conflict. He was already legally fathering two kids.

Anyway, he would help to see that we weren't sent back after my scholarship.

Life abroad is better... he said.

Each time he visited me on campus in my absence, he would leave messages which read as follows:

"Tell her *her husband* was here"......

So funny. It was logical, he couldn't live with me on campus, so we decided he helped me to rent an off-campus accommodation where I and Elina stayed during weekends and school vacations.

He helped me to get a nanny to take care of Elina and every weekend he stayed with us.

We got intimate and he warned sternly that he didn't want any more kids.

"I have enough already," .....he said.

This sounded very pleasant in my ears. Kids are a gift from God but not being married made them seem like a curse.

My neighbours saw Kess as my husband.

Two years went by. Fidelis went back to Nigeria because it was compulsory to return home after the scholarship program.

Elina and I didn't go back because Kess was our guarantor for prolonged stay in Switzerland.

While in Switzerland, I had called Fr. Christopher to thank him dearly and also asked the possibilities of helping to send my son Ngozi to join us in Switzerland.

It wasn't an easy task but Ngozi finally came to join us.

I got a job to manage my little family.

The little flat Kess rented wasn't big enough anymore for us.

I didn't see Kess more often as I wished. Things later changed, maybe because of the arrival of my son. I wasn't happy anymore.

If I have to continue staying here in Switzerland, it would mean that Kess should come and live with me and this was very impossible.

Kess had told me from the very beginning that he couldn't leave his family for me and I on the other hand couldn't date any other man right there in Switzerland to avoid jealousy from Kess because he was my guarantor.

The opportunity came. I applied online for a job with a company in Switzerland, I was given the job but I would have to travel to the branch office in France.

I accepted the offer and we moved to France.

It was there I met Bright.

I didn't know how it happened but I remember after work one day I was rushing to submit some papers at the bank.

I rushed into the elevator and I didn't even notice the people who were in before me.

The language was a barrier; it was only enough for me to say *"Bonjour"* (In French meaning good day) and then smiled afterwards.

Suddenly, I overheard the two black men in the lift talking about disrespect.

"Oh boy....see how this babe fine"...one of them said in pidgin English (meaning : this girl is beautiful) referring to me.

The other one replied,

"Don't mind her, if it is in Nigeria now, she would kneel down to greet."

"See how she said Bonjour to us.."

They were talking and smiling at the same time, not knowing that I understood the language they spoke.

I rushed out of the elevator and was waiting to take a bus to the bank when I heard the honking sound of a car horn.

The driver was Bright, he came to pick up his two colleagues who were studying the French language at the same building where I worked.

I actually didn't notice him, I ignored the call when suddenly the car pulled over and the driver came out.

"Gold," he shouted,

"*Na you be dat*?" He asked in pidgin English (meaning: is that you?)

"Yes, how may I help you?"

"It is Bright, your Bright, can't you remember?

Bright from the Provision stores in Warri."

"Efian (*sic*) Ebobore " I replied...(words expressing surprise in our language).

"Oh what a life..

How are you?

And what are you doing here?" I asked, still short of words, especially in my language.

Bright was still very illiterate. He told me he heard how a lot of our Nigerian girls were prostituting abroad. Although he dated prostitutes, he never wanted to marry them.

"So you study for master's abroad?" He asked.

"*Na wa*," he continued loudly....(meaning: surprised)

"*Shuo*? (*slang* to accompany a surprise)

Effurun, see *Warri* ," he shouted. He behaved very barbaric. (Effurun is a town Delta State, Nigeria)

"It was my colleagues who pointed at you, I didn't see you," he continued.

He asked his colleagues to get out of his car because according to him, he was taking his woman (that would be me) to where ever she is heading.

I begged him to drop them off first and he could take me to the bank afterwards.

He accepted gladly.

And it was then we started our little affair.

I got to learn slowly that he was very fraudulent. He had a very beautiful car and he wore a lot of expensive. He was had a Rolex watch on. On the other days, he had other

designers on like Gucci, Prada and so on.

He worked as a painter and he had a lot of skeleton in his cupboard.

On this particular date, I went visiting his apartment. We cooked together and we made love. It was really intimate, not like I ever had before or what I'd fantasized.

It was after sex he told me he didn't mind if I had two kids from two different men.

"You see my dear, hmmm…." he said,

"I have been in Erope," (I corrected him, Europe)

"Ehen, Urope, he mistakenly repeated again.

I have not seen any woman who came from Nigeria to study.

All of them *na ashawo*…… (*slang* : meaning they are all prostitute)

I don't mind going to pay your bride price ooooo

I want to marry youooooo," he shouted while having our traditional music playing loudly on his CD player.

I replied, "Ok ooooooo," in unison.

Then we both laughed.

And our relationship continued without problems until one day I visited him again unexpectedly (because I had visited once, not being expected but he wasn't home) and I saw all

the evidences I needed to confirm my suspicion.

He was a 419'er (also known as the 419 scam after the section of the Nigerian criminal code dealing with fraud), so it was impossible to continue any kind of relationship with

him. He was the only one I didn't introduce as my husband. Although he had his good side (being generous, always giving to the needy), there wasn't any need.

I continued working and at the same time praying hard for a husband.

I was promoted at my office and I had to move from my rented apartment to a house.

I needed help to move. Firstly, I had to pack every of our belongings into cartons and then organize the transporting vehicles.

I had to do these all on my own, luckily my kids were away at school.

I was moving from one place to the other to find some help when I met some lady (Veroniqué) from my church. She told me about a centre where a lot of Africans without

resident permit come together.

I actually had stuffs to give away. I could hire a moving company but it was too expensive.

I was going to give away my washing-machine, my oven, some old clothes and for this, I would have to pay to the moving company to help throw them away.

I explained to Veroniqué and she persuaded me not to patronize the moving company.

"En fait , à cette adresse que je vous donne maintenant , she insisted in French meaning in English "In fact, go to this address I am giving you now,"

"Merci, au revoir," I replied.

"Ils aideront à vous aider à déplacer et vous leur donner ces choses en retour gratuitement meaning in English "They will assist in helping you move and you give them these things in return for free," she concluded.

I took a day off from work to enable me visit the address Veroniqué gave me.

Instead of visiting the centre that day, I went to the shop to buy nail polish.

It was summer and I had a lot of summer shoes I needed to put on but because my nails weren't nicely polish, I always had the wrong shoes on.

'So today I will go and buy polish', I told myself while glancing at my mirror.

One thing led to the other, I ended up only polishing my nails and not going to the centre that day.

Fortunately, the next day I stopped working at 12noon; I took off after work and went to the centre.

It was then I met Benjamin.

It was me who recognized him because he was smartly dressed. Benjamin didn't change facially at all, like all the other men I met several years after. That day he had a Michael

Kors shirt on. He was distinct from the crowd.

According to him, he worked at the centre as a volunteer and he never worked on Wednesdays, only half days on Thursdays, he was on his way home when I bumped into him. It

seemed spiritually right because I had gone to buy my nail polish on Wednesday and Thursday I had gone in search of help and I met him.

If I had gone on Wednesday, I would have met the director who was going to point out some men at the centre to help me move and bring back the donations I had to the centre.

So you see again? What a coincidence!

"Hello," I said.

"Do you remember me?" I continued.

"No," he replied sarcastically.

"I am Gold, you used to sell " Okrika" at the university in Nigeria then, and sorry to ask, how did you come abroad? I mean am really sorry to ask."

"Oh, is that you?" He said.

"Hi, nice to meet you," he continued. He stood up to greet me properly.

Back then, even though I was poor, each time I went to his second hand shop, I would always ask for new things. It was then he took note of me. He also had new clothes in his

second hand shop, that made it very interesting for me because they weren't so expensive as they were in other shops.

"Please let's sit down and talk," he continued.

"I went back to Ghana to settle down after a few years of selling Okrika. The new Vice Chancellor at the University discontinued sales at the entrance to the school, all the shops

were sent packing, so I left.

I have 3 kids and my wife left me because I was still too poor for her.

I didn't actually mind, I struggled very hard to please her, but she grew too fat and became so unkempt. I just had to leave her. My kids are now with my family and she left with

her boyfriend.

I came abroad by foot. I walked through the desert and through the Moroccan-Spain river and here I am in France," he said in narrative.

It was summer, I had very little clothes on. My nipples were transparent. And I wasn't fat and I wasn't so smartly dressed.

And he ? He looked like a model.

I finally learnt that he hasn't got legitimate papers to stay in France even though he was being harboured by a French woman.

She had Ben at home only for sex and cleaning her apartment. Nothing else.

Painful, I thought. He is playing slave to some woman and here I am, needing help….. I thought in my heart..

"Why are you here?" He asked

"I am moving, and I have some things to donate to this centre. I got the address from a lady called Veroniqué.

She told me people at this centre can make use of anything because they are very poor, is that true?" I asked smiling.

"I just got promoted and I got a new place with every modern convenience in it so I wouldn't be needing some of my stuff like the washing machine and so on," I replied him.

"Ok, no problems, I can help you move."

My kids were away at the summer playschool on the day he visited me.

We got talking and one thing led to the other he demanded for sex.

I refused totally. Although he was a little bit my kind of man, I just said 'no'.

I have been abroad for a while now and from all I have seen, a lot of girls here are promiscuous (I mean no offence).

They could have sex everywhere, often times without protection, they give blow jobs called "cock-sucking" under the office tables to managers and colleagues.

Knowing how enlightened I am, if these men have sexually transmitted disease like HIV, or Chlamydia and so on, these girls will eventually become infected.

A married white woman doesn't see it as a problem giving blow jobs at the office or even have office sex, in fact they enjoyed it. It was part of socializing and an item in the office culture.

It had recently been announced on radio that the percentage of sexually transmitted disease is on the increase.

People claim they use condom while having sex, what about while giving blow jobs?

A number of these men are uncircumcised and the uncircumcised penis is a breeding ground for sexual infections according to online reports I read on www.circinfo.net.

So with that thought in mind, I refused intimacy with Ben.

I took him to my house doctor and he was confirmed with Chlamydia and Herpes.

Even though I bought medications for him so he could get treated of Chlamydia infection, he wasn't prepared to leave Peri, his white girlfriend. She was paying him. I wasn't

ready to pay him to stay with me.

So his idea was he would visit me regularly and still stay with her.

Ben was also an illiterate.

I questioned him one day on our date together.

"Are you still intimate with Peri, after being cured of Chlamydia, with Herpes still left untreated, have you asked her to get checked?"

"She is the reason for the Chlamydia, and be careful, maybe some other infections soon, because they are very promiscuous here, without self-control or restrictions.

The women here enjoy sex like Christmas holidays....I warn you."

"Oh Peri is not like that," he replied me.

"Ok stay with her. I can't become infected." I reiterated.

"Don't you know that after cure, you can become re-infected if you are still with the same partner?"

"Ha, is that so?" He asked.

"Ok then, I won't sleep with her anymore." He said sadly.

He lied to me. He was still sleeping with her, that is the reason he got paid monthly.

Deep down in his heart, he was in pain. He wasn't happy.

Even though he liked me the way I was, he needed money. He would do anything for money and I wasn't prepared to take any risk with him.

He was lusting after me and I just couldn't give in.

His only problem was money and legal papers to stay in France.

I could provide all these for him knowing how successful I am. Although I didn't let him know how much I earned monthly, being with him would mean "checking on him" every

time.

Why was I afraid then? The way he talked about money meant that he would flee away with the highest bidder, any woman who is ready to pay him would be lucky to have him.

But after all these while with him, even though I had the cause to introduce him to my neighbours in my new place of abode as my husband, I found him to be a liar and cheat.

So what next?

Who is my husband then?

I have also occasionally met some white guys who had taken interest in me, I didn't object to their interest, that is why I had written in red "maybe Benjamin is not the one meant to complete my story, maybe probably a white guy."

Epilogue

JOHN CHAPTER 4:18 (King James Version of the bible)

When Jesus was at the well, he asked the woman he met to give him water and thereafter.

Jesus told her "Go call thy husband."

She replied "I have none," even though according to the bible passage she has had five husbands, Jesus was so Holy to ask her "where is your husband?"

It would have been rude to address her as a prostitute , rather Jesus was kind to her.

The word "many (5) husbands" was first used in the bible.

In the African tradition, a man can marry as many women as he chooses, but my question is:

Why can't a woman do the same in Africa? Polyandry is accepted in some parts of the world, why not everywhere? Who was the brain behind

 polygamy in the African tradition? Whoever or whatever it was didn't also think about polyandry? This would have made a number of women

happier based on the interview I had with some ladies who claimed they are living in bondage in their various marriages.

What does God our Creator think about polyandry? Has anybody cared to find out?

Such a knowledge would have been very wonderful for me because I have experienced everything unique and different from each of these

different men I mentioned in my story.

It would have been so ideal to be able to switch from one man to the other while married to all of them just like the polygamist.

Mr. Right

"Who is Mr. Right?" That name becomes popular on the lips of many women who have, in the past been involved in various dating relationships.

These women have experienced something unique in the different men in these relationships until finally they meet a new man having all these

unique qualities in one body.

After marrying Mr. Right, what we later read on the lips of these "Mrs.'s Right" is that they want a divorce….the Mr. Right they got married to is

actually not Mr. Right anymore, a shortcoming in the marriage is experienced at a later stage of the marriage.

What does this conclude? According to one of the responses I gathered from my interview "I would love to marry Mr. Right in addition to Mr.

Solution to the shortcomings in my marriage." One of the ladies concluded.

With the qualities of being romantic, generous, fun loving etc. in one man still not enough for Mrs. Right, what would be more ideal then? Does it mean that Mrs. Right is insatiable? Or women in general are insatiable?

Frankly speaking, taking a look at the life of a woman, she suffers a lot, she is the one who menstruates monthly, often times the symptoms of menstruation are very painful, she carries a child for 9 months in her womb, the pain at child birth is indescribable, and sometimes, more often than not, she is left with the issues of running a home and so on. With these kind of pains, can the woman's insatiability be justified?

I am a woman though I cannot use the verb insatiable in qualifying myself, but there are times when I feel like I just being romantic alone, then I'd switch to Ken, and talking about benevolence and generosity, I would gladly switch hands between Iyke and Bright and then when I need help to get my garbage organized then I'd call Benjamin.

My life is not justified, I see myself as a sinner. I have the means enough to invite the two men in Africa to come to France to marry me now that am about to make it official,

who will I marry amongst all these men including these other 3 (I am willing to change Bright into a better person) in Europe?

Till today, Ken the father of my first child is a divorcee, he has contacted me so many times about us continuing our romance but I would have

none of it and then Iyke who left me for Onyinye. Although still legally married to Onyin, is ready to divorce her and come abroad again to marry

me because according to him he showed me benevolence but with Onyin whom was a kind of complete stranger to him, he showed nothing. In

fact he'd beat her up each time there was a quarrel, quarrel about having kids, because till date, they are still childless (she was actually pregnant once, but she lost it), Elina my daughter is his only child now.

Onyinye couldn't pack her things out of the marriage because Igbo marriage is like some kind of institution I would like to term "NON REFUNDABLE or NON RETURNABLE" (I mean no offence).

According to the Igbo custom, and according to the little information I have, the men "buy" the women for a kind of ridiculous price (I mean no offence). The bride prices differ, for an illiterate to a highly schooled woman.

Sometimes, the women involved are from poor families making it difficult for them after divorce to be able to return the bride prices paid on them.

It was indeed some sort of non- refundable situation for Onyinye and Iyke , but he was willing to forget it all and move to France for me.

On the other hand, Kess was willing to make me his African wife but it would mean that I and my kids may not see him at some important holidays

like Christmas because of his Oyinbo wife Ana. I cannot play a second fiddle to anyone. God forbid!

Bright, a fraudulent 419'er is still roaming the streets of Europe looking for his next victim. He was prepared to marry me, he was prepared to give me the "BIG" wedding I always

desired. According to him, marriage to Goldie would mean everything would come in Gold, he has stolen so much US dollars and European Euros, but come to think of it, is there anything wrong in this? Yes indeed, there are so many things wrong, because I am a woman of integrity, even though I had kids outside wedlock, I cannot afford sleeping without my eyes closed. Each time Bright sees a cop or a police patrol car, his heart skips a beat, the only word that comes out of his mouth then is

"Heeehehhhe, kasala wan burst".. (Nigerian slang: Problems are about to arise).

It is a NO for him but I am willing to transform him.

Benjamin , and all these other men have demonstrated how interested they are in marrying me and I have, in one way or another, and at different circumstances and places introduced them as my husband.

Now, I am about to make it official, who will I chose?

Dear readers please advise me, or I would remain "A woman of many husbands, on lip only and not on paper."

Goldie.

www.ingramcontent.com/pod-product-compliance
Lightning Source LLC
Chambersburg PA
CBHW040846180526
45159CB00001B/333